T0199002

THE BALL

Communicating

By Andie Lee

WestBow Press books may be ordered through booksellers or by contacting:

WestBow Press
A Division of Thomas Nelson & Zondervan
1663 Liberty Drive
Bloomington, IN 47403
www.westbowpress.com
844-714-3454

ISBN: 979-8-3850-0378-5 (sc)
ISBN: 979-8-3850-0379-2 (e)

Library of Congress Control Number: 2023913703

Print information available on the last page.

WestBow Press rev. date: 12/14/2023

WESTBOW
P R E S S®
A DIVISION OF THOMAS NELSON
& ZONDERVAN

**This book is dedicated to God, and
to all the people I love.**

The ball is spoken words.
The ball is communication.

Whoever holds the ball is talking.
(Words have power.)

= When you see this heart above a stick person, it means that the person is trying to communicate, and they are mentally in a good place.

The Listener

The Talker

Good Communication

Listening and Receiving   **Talking**

More Good Communication

The listener catches the ball. They heard what was said. They are now ready to talk.

The talker talked (they threw the ball). They are now ready to listen.

The Good Game

Now talking.   Now listening.

Good Listening Skills

Create a safe space to talk.

Be in the present - not distracted. Be respectful and patient.

Listen VERY well. Maintain eye contact. Don't interrupt.

Try to understand the other person.

Good Talking Skills

Create a safe space to talk.

Be in the present - not distracted. Be respectful and kind.

Speak kind, encouraging words.

Express hurts & challenges honestly without blaming - seek to solve problems as much as possible.

Maintain eye contact.

Strive to speak calmly, clearly, & don't yell.

Some Causes of Communication Fails

The person doesn't feel loved (especially when they were young.)

The person doesn't feel heard.

The person wants to be heard and understood. The person has anxiety and frustrations.

The person has learned to yell, or to use other poor communication skills.

The person explodes (yells or screams) or implodes (hides or withdraws).

Communication Fails

FAIL #1: The Head Spike

The talker responds with mean, angry, unkind words, or actions.

The Listener

FAIL #2: My Ball's Better

The Talker

The listener catches the ball & tosses it away. No response.

Bag of own
balls

**The listener chooses
a new ball.**

The person only talks about themselves or what they think. They're either selfish or are afraid to talk about a topic.

FAIL #3: Hides the Ball

The Talker   **The Listener**

The person hides the ball.
They won't talk because
they're either mad, too afraid
to talk, or are punishing the
other with the silent treatment.

FAIL #4: The Screamer

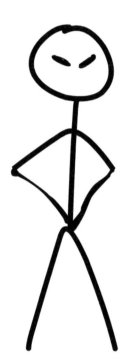 

Tension or anger between both people.

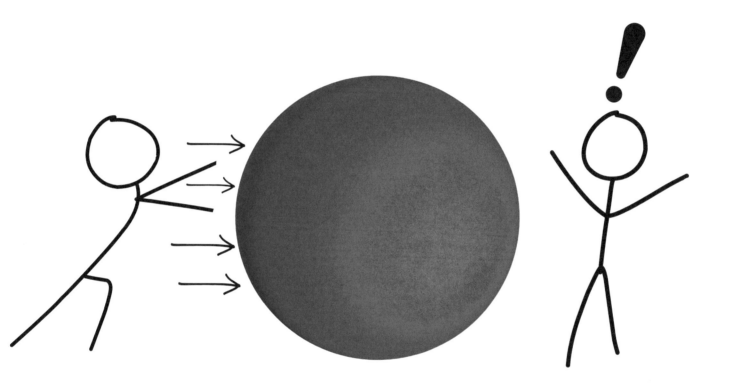

The BIG ball. YELLING. They use very loud, intimidating words to try to control the other person - or the situation.

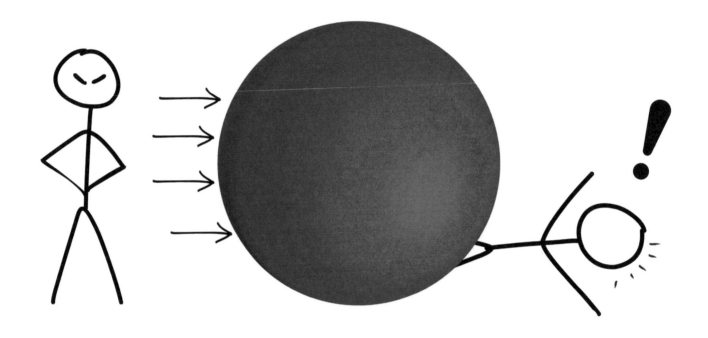

They try to over-power the other person, and often won't let them talk. They want to cause fear in the other person.

FAIL #5: Ghosting (Disappearing)

The person disappears with no explanations.

FAIL #6: Stuck in Your Head (Obsessed)

The person is not communicating because they are over- thinking, obsessing, are paranoid, or are stuck in their own thoughts.

FAIL #7: Detached

The ball is ignored. The person is present, but is not responding. They either don't care, or are suffering from trauma, detachment, or fear.

FAIL #8: Ping-Pong Paddle

The Listener

The person controls the conversation. They bombard the listener with lots of words and won't let the other person talk.

FAIL #9: The Judger

The Talker

The Listener

**Critical. Judges the other person. Controlling.
Uses conditional love - I'll love you,
if you do what I expect.**

FAIL #10: Too Busy - The Workaholic

The Talker

The Listener

The person sets the ball down. They're too busy to talk. They value getting things done - more than the other person.

FAIL #11: Barely There

The Talker　　　　　　**The Listener**

The person barely communicates. They are present, but are distracted. They respond with "uh-huh" or "yep," and have very little eye contact.

FAIL #12: Surprise Darts

These people have a good relationship, except...

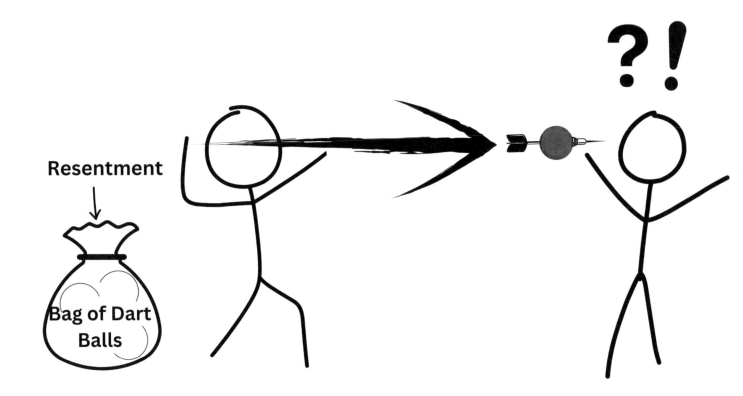

...the other person throws an occasional, unexpected word dart ball -- a sarcastic comment or a quick nasty jab.

Dart balls can be small or "nuclear." Don't let them build up.

Bag of Dart Balls

I need to learn to talk through my problems.

Surprise dart balls are often caused by anger, underlying, hidden bitterness, resentment, or jealousy. This person is not working through problems as they happen. They are stuffing their emotions. They are not talking. They are not forgiving and letting go of the past.

FAIL #13: War

The Spiked Ball

Vicious words. People seek to harm and wound each other deeply.

There is no kindness, no mercy, no love, and no forgiveness.

FAIL #14: Impatient Listener

The person is hearing but is not really listening. They can't wait to talk.

They have many opinions and thoughts they want to express.

And once they get to talk, they bombard the other person with their opinions.

FAIL #15: Speechless

No ball. What do I say to that person?

The Solution

**Learn to ask questions about the other person.
Be interested in them. Care about them.**

FAIL #16: Attack

Bomb Ball

An attack.

The Solution

**This person puts out the flame. They stay calm.
They show love to the other person.**

FAIL #17: Abuse

When someone is playing unfairly, or is being unkind, you don't have to stay in the game.

Be polite and respectful, tell them you love them, that you'll be back, but you're leaving for a while - until they can play nice. You don't have to take abuse.

"Love is patient, love is kind..."

1 Corinthians 13:4 NIV

"Everyone should be quick to listen, slow to speak and slow to become angry..."

James 1:19 NIV

About the Author

Andie Lee has spent nearly 30 years studying God's foods, diets, and health in a variety of arenas. She has a passion for helping others regain their lives. Andie has a degree in Holistic Nutrition and various other certifications in the fields of healing.

Printed in the United States
by Baker & Taylor Publisher Services